Mysterious Encounters

The Possessed

by Craig E. Blohm

KIDHAVEN PRESS
An imprint of Thomson Gale, a part of The Thomson Corporation

THOMSON

GALE

Detroit • New York • San Francisco • New Haven, Conn. • Waterville, Maine • London

© 2008 Thomson Gale, a part of The Thomson Corporation.

Thomson and Star Logo are trademarks and Gale and KidHaven Press are registered trademarks used herein under license.

For more information, contact

KidHaven Press
27500 Drake Rd.
Farmington Hills, MI 48331-3535
Or you can visit our Internet site at http://www.gale.com

LIBRARY OF CONGRESS CATALOGING-IN-PUBLICATION DATA

Blohm, Craig E., 1948-
  The possessed / by Craig E. Blohm.
    p. cm. — (Mysterious encounters)
  Includes bibliographical references and index.
  ISBN-13: 978-0-7377-3781-3 (hardcover)
  1. Spirit possession—Juvenile literature. 2. Demoniac
possession—Juvenile literature. I. Title.
  BF1555.B54 2008
  133.4'26—dc22
 	
                                                              2007022222

ISBN-10: 0-7377-3781-6

Printed in the United States of America

Contents

Chapter 1

Possessed by Spirits

In the late twentieth century, most people did not worry about being possessed by evil spirits. Belief in such things seemed part of an ancient, **superstitious** world. Then, in 1973, a movie got the American public thinking about the spirit world and the possible dangers lurking there. *The Exorcist* told the tale of a twelve-year-old girl whose body was taken over by an evil spirit, or demon. The film showed grotesque changes that the demon inflicted on the girl's body and personality.

Some moviegoers became ill or fainted at seeing the horrifying images on the screen. Many began to fear that possession might actually be true. This fear intensified when it was revealed that *The Exorcist* was based on a true story.

Reports of possession have been made for thousands of years. For many, these accounts confirm the existence of a spirit world that exists undetected by us in our everyday lives. Undetected, that is, until a spirit enters the physical world through an unsuspecting person.

What Is Possession?

Possession, sometimes called spiritual possession, occurs when a spirit enters a person's body and takes control. The spirit may be a **benign** spirit that does no harm to the person it enters. Such a spirit may actually help or comfort a person. But when most people think about possession they think of demons possessing a person. Demonic possession can cause physical and

A possessed person will look strange and act in violent ways as this movie scene suggests.

emotional damage. When someone is possessed by a demon, his or her personality, behavior, and sometimes appearance may drastically change. For example, a normally quiet person might become loud and aggressive and use foul language. Possessed people often exhibit great physical strength, violent behavior, and multiple personalities.

Many experts think the disturbing actions of people who believe they are possessed are merely symptoms of mental illness. Others are sure that demons can invade a person, creating the appearance of mental or emotional disturbance. No matter which is true, history shows that belief in demonic possession has been around for a long time.

Possession in Ancient Cultures

Scientist Carl Sagan wrote, "Belief in demons was widespread in the ancient world."[1] The Sumerians believed that illnesses were caused by demon possession.

Archaeologists have found Sumerian tablets containing prayers asking for deliverance from demon possession. In ancient Greece it was thought that spirits could influence peoples' lives even without actual possession. According to the Greek poet Homer, "A sick man pining away is one upon whom an evil spirit has gazed."[2] But the Greeks believed that not all demons were evil. Socrates, a great Greek philosopher, said he was possessed by a benign spirit who guided him and helped him avoid mistakes.

The Bible describes many instances of Jesus driving demons out of the possessed. While traveling near the town of Gadara, Jesus met a man who was possessed by many demons. These demons tortured the man night and day, driving him almost insane. He lived in misery in the tombs near the town. When Jesus commanded

Boars possessed by evil spirits are driven into the sea.

An elderly woman, one of many thought to be possessed, is led away during the Salem witch trials.

the spirits to depart, they left the man and went into a herd of pigs that was grazing nearby. The pigs then rushed down the bank of a lake and drowned.

In another encounter a troubled woman approached Jesus, saying, "Lord, Son of David, have mercy on me. My daughter is suffering terribly from demon-possession."[3] Jesus was impressed by the woman's faith and drove the demon from her daughter.

Spirits in Colonial America

In 1692 in the village of Salem, Massachusetts, two young girls began acting in very strange ways. Betty Parris and Abigail Williams screamed, threw objects, and twisted their bodies into unnatural positions. When Betty's father, the Reverend Samuel Parris, preached, the girls covered their ears. The villagers believed these weird behaviors were "beyond the power of Epileptic Fits or natural disease to effect."[4] Betty and Abigail were thought to be bewitched by evil spirits. Soon other girls began exhibiting similar odd behavior.

Betty and Abigail began accusing many of their neighbors of being witches. A special court was set up to try cases of witchcraft. Scores of people, both women and men, were arrested and put on trial. In six months, twenty people were convicted and hanged. Were the girls really possessed or influenced by spirits? Today some people believe that they were simply "acting out" against the strict morality of the day. As with many paranormal claims, we may never know for sure.

In the 1740s America underwent a religious revival called the Great Awakening. Many people listened to

The Bread of Salem

One theory put forth to explain the strange behavior of the Salem witches leads to the rye fields of the town. Eating rye bread contaminated with a fungus called ergot may have caused hallucinations that were interpreted as bewitching.

powerful preachers and became enthusiastic about their personal relationship with God. But even in this time of growing faith people could still be possessed. In Boston in 1741, 23-year-old Martha Roberson told Joseph Pitkin, a visitor, that the devil "knows You are a Goodman and he hates all such and he will Roar in me anon."[5] For two days, Pitkin talked with Martha about

The Roman Catholic Church has rituals and books that explain how to drive out evil spirits from possessed people.

her spiritual possession. She said that a traveling preacher had put the demon into her, causing her to have a seizure. Pitkin was horrified at the foul language the demon spoke through Martha. At one point she "gave a Loud shriek as Loud as her Voice would Carry it."[6]

When Pitkin visited Martha two years later, she seemed to be no longer possessed. There is no record of how or when the demon left her. But Pitkin kept a diary of his encounter with the possessed woman, and it still exists today.

Possession Today

Belief in spiritual possession is widespread even in our modern world. The Roman Catholic Church has rituals for driving out evil spirits. In numerous Protestant denominations physical signs of a person being filled with God's Holy Spirit are central to faith and worship. Many African and Caribbean religions also incorporate spiritual possession into their ceremonies. These spirits may be good or evil, or may be the ghosts of departed friends or relatives.

There are **skeptics** who do not believe that spirits and spiritual possession exist. They offer natural explanations for the sometimes frightening actions of those who believe they are possessed. Skeptic Robert Todd Carroll says that "the behaviors of the possessed resemble very closely the behaviors of those with . . . physical or emotional disorders."[7] Science has not been able to prove the existence of

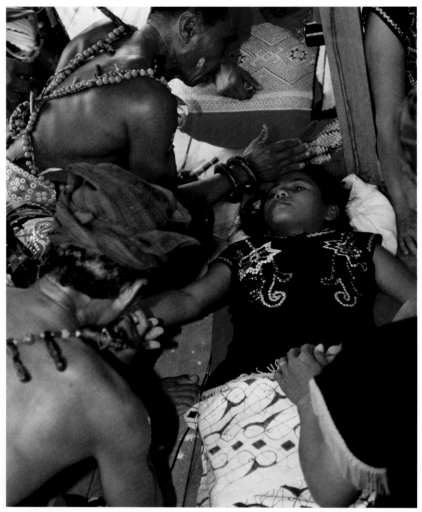

A witch doctor performs an exorcism in Indonesia.

spiritual possession, but neither has it demonstrated that possession is not real. Stories of spiritual possession continue to fascinate many people around the world. If these stories are true, they point to an invisible realm inhabited by spirits that can either help the human race—or fill it with terror.

Chapter 2

Contacting the Spirit World

Many people have tried to contact beings who reside in the spirit world. Some wish to talk to loved ones who have died. Others believe they can receive knowledge from the spirits of wise people who lived thousands of years ago. Despite skeptics who question the reality of such contact, opening the door to "the other side" has long been a popular pastime.

Séances in the Lincoln White House

The mid-19th century saw the rise of the spiritualist movement in the United States. In many large cities people called mediums set up shop. Mediums

Mary Todd Lincoln (pictured) tried to contact the spirit of her deceased son.

claimed to have the ability to communicate with the spirits of the departed. They held séances, in which a group of people sat around a table in a darkened room. The medium went into a **trance** and invited a spirit to make contact through her. The spirit then took over the medium's body. Many people were comforted to hear from departed loved ones and know that their spirits lived on.

Some historians say that President Abraham Lincoln had an interest in spiritualism that helped him cope with the demands of his presidency and the Civil War. As a young man, Lincoln once told a friend that he "always had a strong tendency to mysticism."[8] He often had dreams that seemed to predict the future. But it was Lincoln's wife, Mary Todd, who earnestly sought to communicate with the spirit world.

In 1862 the Lincolns' eleven-year-old son, Willie, died following a short illness. After Willie's death, Mary tried to contact the spirit of her beloved son through séances. Orville Browning, a family friend, wrote that Mary went "to see a Mrs. Laury, a spiritualist and she had made wonderful revelations to her about her little son Willy who died last winter."[9] As many as eight séances may have been held in the White House during Lincoln's presidency.

In early 1863 Lincoln's army was having a difficult time on the battlefield. During a séance a medium named Nettie Maynard contacted a spirit named Dr. Bamford. Through the medium, Bamford described for the president the dire condition of the Union army. The spirit told Lincoln that a personal visit to the battlefield would encourage his troops. Lincoln did so, and later that year the

Abraham Lincoln is said to have visited troops on the advice of a spirit summoned during the Civil War.

Union army achieved a critical victory in the Battle of Gettysburg. The tide of the war shifted and the Confederate forces were eventually defeated.

Did advice from a spirit really help save the United States? Skeptics contend that séances are nothing more than scams to fool the **gullible**. But even today, Abraham Lincoln's own spirit is said to wander though the White House.

Messages from the Ouija Board

A Ouija board is a wooden board upon which are printed the letters of the alphabet. A small heart-shaped pointer, called a planchette, is placed on the Ouija board. When one or more people lightly rest their fingers on the planchette, it mysteriously moves across the board. The letters it points to are said to spell out messages from the spirit world. By the early 20th century, the Ouija board had become a popular fad.

Pearl Curran lived with her husband, John, in St. Louis, Missouri. Although Pearl and her friends occasionally played with a Ouija board, it was always just for fun. On the evening of July 8, 1913, Pearl and a neighbor were sitting with a Ouija board on their laps, their fingers touching the planchette. Suddenly, the pointer began to move, spelling out: "Many moons ago I lived. I come again. Patience Worth my name. . . . I would speak with thee. If thou shalt live, then so shall I."[10]

Pearl learned that Patience Worth was a Quaker woman who had lived in England around 1649. Patience began sending Pearl messages through the Ouija board. Eventually there were so many long messages that Pearl had to stop using the board because it was too slow. She began dictating the wisdom of Patience Worth to her husband, who wrote furiously to keep up.

Through Pearl, Patience communicated many thousands of words, including wise sayings, plays, hundreds of poems, and six

Many people use Ouija boards in their attempts to contact the spirit world.

novels. Among her literary works were the historical novels *The Sorry Tale* and *Hope Trueblood*. Within these writings was evidence that convinced many people that spirit communication was indeed taking place. The language Patience used was an **archaic** form of English spoken in the seventeenth century. Her writing showed knowledge of English animals, trees, and flowers, as well as the way of life in England in the 1600s. These were things that Pearl Curran, a poorly educated high school dropout, would not be likely to know.

By 1922 Pearl was receiving fewer messages from Patience. By the time Pearl died in 1937, all communication from Patience had ceased, and the public had long forgotten the 17th-century literary genius who spoke through a simple St. Louis housewife.

A Channel to the Other Side

Some people claim the power to convey important information to us by becoming a channel, or link, between the spirit world and our world. Channelers say they have received teachings from many individuals, including Jesus, Buddha, angels, and even aliens from space.

Judy Zebra Knight always believed that she possessed **psychic** powers. In 1977 J.Z. (as she had come to be called), then a housewife and cable TV executive, was in her kitchen when a 7-foot-tall (2.1m) entity appeared to her. He said, "Beloved woman, I am Ramtha the Enlightened One, and I have come to help you. . . . I am here, and we are going to do grand work together."[11] Ramtha told her that he was a warrior who lived on Earth 35,000 years ago in the ancient land of Lemuria, a supposedly lost continent in the Pacific Ocean.

Ramtha chose Knight as the channel through which he would bring his ancient wisdom to the modern world. According to Knight, being a channel is different than acting as a medium. While a spirit makes contact through a medium, in channeling the spirit actually inhabits the channeler's body. Knight learned how to spiritually leave her body so that Ramtha could enter. She describes it as being "like a death process. I go through a tunnel and there's a whistling sound and a light at the end. As soon as I hit the light I come back."[12] By the mid-1980s Knight had become one of the most famous channelers in the world.

A channeler acts as a link to the spirit world.

When Knight channels, she goes into a trance and begins speaking in the voice of Ramtha. While in Knight's body, Ramtha talks in a husky, slightly accented English. His message is one of personal enlightenment, teaching that God is within every human being, and that every person can create his or her own reality. Ramtha says that God "is the basis of the fulfillment of all your dreams. But who is the dream-maker? You. And what are your dreams made of? Thought, God, life."[13]

Chapter 3

Cases of Possession

Not all encounters with the spirit world result in helpful advice or creative literary works. The annals of **parapsychology** are filled with enough stories of haunted houses and ghostly apparitions to chill the bravest soul. But when a spirit takes over a person's body and personality, the result can be the most frightening experience anyone can imagine.

The Devil in Elizabeth Knapp

Sixteen-year-old Elizabeth Knapp was a servant in the home of Reverend Samuel Willard, the minister of the colonial town of Groton, Massachusetts. In 1671 Elizabeth began to exhibit some alarming behavior that made many in the town believe that she was possessed. Willard kept a written record of Elizabeth's encounter with the devil.

According to Willard, Elizabeth experienced fits "in which she was violent in bodily motions . . . in roarings and screamings, representing a dark resemblance of hellish torments."[14] She grasped her throat, claiming that someone was strangling her. She would give off horrible shrieks followed by periods of seemingly uncontrollable laughter. During some of Elizabeth's fits it took six men to hold her down. She told Willard that the devil had appeared

While Elizabeth Knapp was possessed, she shocked townspeople with her odd and alarming behavior.

to her because she was unhappy being poor. Satan, she said, offered her wealth and an end to her life of hard work.

A physician was called in, but he could do nothing to help her. Although the minister prayed for Elizabeth, her actions grew worse. She hit and spit in the faces of those trying to restrain her during her convulsions. When the devil spoke through Elizabeth, her throat swelled to the size of a man's fist. She called Willard "a great black rogue" who "tell[s] the people a company of lies."[15] The reverend knew it was the devil speaking through Elizabeth and replied, "Satan, thou art a liar and a deceiver, and God will vindicate his own truth one day."[16] When told that God had him in chains, he replied, "For all my chains, I can knock thee in the head when I please."[17]

Elizabeth remained possessed for at least three months after her fits began. Then Willard's written remarks end. History tells us nothing more about the young girl, except that she married and that she died at the age of 65. Was she really possessed by the devil? Or was she simply acting out her dissatisfaction with a poor working girl's life in a most dramatic manner? Only Elizabeth Knapp—and perhaps the devil himself—know the answer.

The Watseka Wonder

In July 1877 thirteen-year-old Lurancy Vennum collapsed and fell into a trance at her home in the

Lurancy Vennum (pictured) spoke in strange voices and took on the personality of another young girl.

small Illinois town of Watseka. Although unconscious, she was able to tell her family that she was in heaven and saw, among other spirits, her brother who had died three years before. For six months Lurancy had several spells a day, suffering from abdominal pains and speaking in strange voices. Some spells lasted up to eight hours, after which Lurancy awoke, remembering nothing. News of the girl's bizarre spells soon spread throughout the town.

When Asa Roff heard about Lurancy's strange behavior, he became interested in the young girl's illness. Roff visited the Vennum home accompanied by Dr. E. W. Stevens, who hypnotized Lurancy. She told of being taken over by evil spirits, including that of a young man who had committed suicide. When the doctor asked if there were any good spirits that she might let control her instead, she mentioned several names, including one in particular: Mary Roff. "That is my daughter," Asa Roff

A Life from the Past

Was the possession of Lurancy Vennum a case of reincarnation? Many people feel they have lived as another person in a past life. But experts say that false memories or information once learned but since forgotten can account for most accounts of reincarnation.

exclaimed. "Mary Roff is my girl. . . . Yes, let her come."[18] He explained that he had become interested in Lurancy's illness because Mary had died of a similar malady twelve years before.

By the next day Lurancy had, in effect, become Mary Roff. She had no memory of her life as Lurancy Vennum, and did not recognize her own family. She wanted only to go home—to the Roff house. When Asa Roff's wife and his daughter, who was named Minerva, came to visit, Lurancy exclaimed, "Here comes Ma and Nervie."[19] Nervie was Mary's nickname for Minerva, and there was no way Lurancy could have known it.

Hoping that Lurancy might get better, her parents allowed her to go with the Roffs. Lurancy knew all the details of the Roff house, although she had never been there before. She remembered incidents that had taken place in Mary's life. She knew Mary's friends by name and recognized clothes, letters, and other items that had been dear to Mary. For three months Lurancy lived as Mary with the Roff family, who were overjoyed to think they had their daughter back. But it would not last. When Lurancy moved in with the Roffs, she predicted that "the angels will let me stay till sometime in May."[20]

In May 1878 Lurancy's old identity began to reassert itself, and she knew it was time to leave the Roffs. She bid a tearful goodbye to the Roffs, their neighbors, and the friends that had known Mary. By the time she went home on May 21, all traces of Mary were gone and Lurancy once more recognized the Vennums and her old home. Lurancy Vennum later married and lived a long and happy life. Stevens spent eight years lecturing about Lurancy Vennum, whom he called the "Watseka Wonder." And what of Mary Roff? Her restless spirit must have finally found peace, for she never reappeared.

The DJ and the Familiar Spirit

Jamsie Z. grew up in New York, the son of an Armenian father and Greek mother. He lived an ordinary early childhood, going to baseball games with his father and saying nightly prayers with his mother. When he was ten years old, however, strange visions began. He began seeing a vision of what he called a "funny-lookin' face."[21] It frightened him so much that he ran home in a panic. As

Jamsie Z was so tortured by demonic possession that he almost took his life at the Pinnacles National Monument (shown).

the vision reappeared through the years, Jamsie became less frightened of the face and more curious.

When he was 23 years old Jamsie began a career as a disc jockey. He worked at radio stations in several cities, finally settling in California. One evening, as Jamsie pulled into his driveway after work, he heard a voice telling him, "Oh, for Pete's sake, Jamsie! Stop acting the fool. We've been together for years. Don't tell me you don't know me."[22] Jamsie did indeed know him—he was the spirit that had been within him since he was a boy. "Well, so long, Jamsie!" the voice said. "See you tomorrow. Wait for your Uncle Ponto."[23] Finally, Jamsie's vision had a name: Uncle Ponto.

Uncle Ponto was a familiar, a spirit that attempts to gain a foothold in a person until it totally shares the person's consciousness. To someone possessed with a familiar, it is like having a twin inside his or her head. Thoughts, feelings, and imaginings occur that are not the person's own, yet the he or she is always aware of them. For a while, the spirit of Uncle Ponto actually helped Jamsie, providing him with a stream of amusing banter that made Jamsie's radio show popular.

But Jamsie's newfound popularity made Ponto angry and jealous. One day Jamsie felt a pain coursing through his body. When the pain subsided, Jamsie heard a familiar voice. "You see, pal," scolded Uncle Ponto. "You already belong to me in great part."[24] Ponto was losing control of Jamsie, and would try to keep it any way he could. Ponto's attacks increased until Jamsie was bombarded with a constant stream of chatter and demands to let Ponto take control. Finally, Jamsie could no longer stand the torture. He jumped into his car and began driving south toward Pinnacles National Monument. The tall peaks and deep canyons there would make an ideal place for Jamsie to jump to his death, ending his demonic torture. When Jamsie reached the monument, Ponto's voice mocked him. "Get it over

One Body, Many Persons

Multiple personality disorder (MPD) is a mental illness in which a person displays not only his own personality, but those of one or more other people as well. Many cases of apparent possession may actually be MPD.

with," the demon urged. "Go on Jamsie! An ideal place for it! . . . Go on, fool! Jump!"[25]

But Jamsie did not jump. A tiny spark of the human instinct for survival now broke through. As he gazed at the beauty of landscape around him, he knew he could not disgrace it with his dead body. He left the monument and called a priest. Together they eventually rid Jamsie of Uncle Ponto, the demon that had possessed him for most of his life.

Chapter 4

Freeing the Possessed

People who are possessed by a demon desperately want to be free of the evil spirit that has invaded their body. This can be done through a ritual called **exorcism**. Performed by a trained exorcist, this dramatic procedure has helped many people rid themselves of their demons.

An Exorcism in Iowa

As a young girl, Emma Schmidt regularly attended church and received Holy Communion. But when she was fourteen years old, she found she could no longer go to church or even pray. Something inside her was preventing her from practicing the faith she loved. Inner voices tormented her, urging her to do

During her exorcism, Emma Schmidt reportedly rose from her bed and flew across the room.

terrible things. Twenty-six years later, the church finally determined that Emma was possessed by demons. Father Theophilus Riesinger, an experienced exorcist, was selected to perform an exorcism. He chose a convent in the small town of Earling, Iowa, as the location for the exorcism to reduce the possibility of publicity and embarrassment for Emma.

Emma was placed on an iron bed in a large room in the convent. As Father Theophilus began the exorcism ritual, Emma became unconscious, her eyes tightly shut. According to nuns in attendance, Emma then suddenly rose from the bed and flew across the room, clinging to the wall high above the door. The shocked nuns forced Emma from the wall and returned her to the bed. She then began howling like a pack of wild animals, wailing so loudly that all hope of secrecy was gone. Crowds began to gather around the convent.

As Father Theophilus prayed over Emma, her body became horribly deformed, her eyes bulging and her lips swelling to twice their normal size. At times she floated above the bed, and at others she weighed down the iron bedstead until it seemed it would break. Father Theophilus realized that several demons were inside Emma. "Who," he asked, "is the leader or prince among you?" The answer came in a deep, raspy voice: "Beelzebub."[26]

The grueling exorcism sessions lasted from morning until night. Eventually, the exorcism began to have an effect on the demons. "Oh, we cannot bear it any longer," they howled. "We suffer intensely." Father Theophilus replied, "Therefore, depart at once, ye cursed. . . . Let this poor woman in peace!"[27] On the twenty-third day, the demons left Emma, chanting their names as they receded

Exorcisms have been done by the Catholic Church for centuries and are sometimes still done today.

34 The Possessed

into the distance and vanished. Emma opened her eyes, and for the first time in years could rejoice, "My Jesus, Mercy! Praised be Jesus Christ!"[28]

The Exorcism of Anneliese Michel

Sometimes an exorcism can have tragic consequences, as in the case of a young woman named Anneliese Michel. The first sign that something was wrong with Anneliese occurred in 1968. Sixteen years old at the time, she began to have uncontrollable fits of shaking that left her unable to cry for help. Anneliese had visions of horrible faces when she prayed, and her behavior became increasingly bizarre. She ate spiders, flies, and pieces of coal, and destroyed religious objects such as crucifixes and pictures of Jesus.

A scene from a movie shows the bizarre events that can occur during an exorcism.

Doctors diagnosed Anneliese with **epilepsy**, but her parents disagreed. They believed that their daughter was possessed. For several years they tried to convince the church to authorize an exorcism for Anneliese. But the church always refused, accepting the medical opinion of the doctors. In the meantime Anneliese continued to suffer, often tearing her clothes, screaming, and hitting members of her family.

Finally the church decided to allow an exorcism, and in September 1975, the exorcism began. Two priests, Father Arnold Renz and Father Ernst Alt,

Like Anneliese Michel, people sometimes claim to be possessed by many personalities.

Exorcism on Trial

Two years after Anneliese Michel died, her parents and the two priests went on trial for causing the girl's death. Doctors testified that epilepsy and mental illness made Anneliese think she was possessed. If she had been given food and medication, they said, she would have lived. The court agreed and sentenced the Michels and the priests to six months in jail.

conducted one or two sessions each week. They soon learned the identities of several demons in Anneliese. She claimed to be possessed by the spirits of Adam and Eve's son Cain, and the Roman emperor Nero, among others. The exorcism sessions were grueling both for the priests and for Anneliese. She exhibited such strength that she often had to be restrained by chains.

But the sessions seemed to be working. Anneliese returned to school for a short time. But soon the demonic attacks returned and Anneliese became even worse. For weeks she refused to eat and lost an alarming amount of weight. She became so weak that she had to be supported by her parents when it was time to kneel for prayers. By

June 1976, Anneliese was literally wasting away from lack of food. Father Renz and Father Alt continued the exorcism rites, praying that Anneliese would soon be healed. But healing would not occur. On July 1, 1976, 23-year-old Anneliese Michel died of starvation. Her last words were, "Mother, I'm afraid."[29]

Perhaps Anneliese Michel really was possessed, but her death was the result of drastic measures taken to rid her of her demons. In 1999 the Catholic Church approved a new exorcism rite that cautions exorcists to avoid confusing possession with mental illness. It was the first new exorcism manual to be issued since 1614.

The True Story of The Exorcist

People who attended the 1973 movie *The Exorcist* saw the story of a little girl possessed by a terrifying demon. Few of these moviegoers knew the real story that inspired the film. If truth is sometimes stranger than fiction, it can also be just as frightening.

Robbie was thirteen years old in 1949 when mysterious occurrences surrounding him began. Robbie's family heard strange scratching and tapping noises in their Maryland house. Soon objects began to move by themselves and even fly across Robbie's room. His bed shook and he screamed as nightmares tortured him. Bloody scratches appeared on his body, and his normal personality changed as he became angry and violent.

Desperate to find relief for their son, Robbie's parents took him to a Catholic church. Father Edward Hughes prayed for Robbie and gave his parents holy water and blessed candles. When Robbie's torment continued, Father Hughes was convinced that the boy was possessed and decided to conduct an exorcism in a Washington, D.C., hospital. A report stated that "the hospital bed rammed all the way across the room, all by itself. Scratch marks would suddenly appear on his [Robbie's] chest while nuns were looking on."[30]

The Exorcist was based on the possession and subsequent exorcism of Robbie Mannheim.

Father Hughes's exorcism was unsuccessful, so Robbie's parents thought moving might rid their son of his demon. One night Robbie's mother found the word "Louis" scratched in blood on Robbie's chest. She considered this a sign, for she had relatives in St. Louis, Missouri. The change of location did not help, however, so another exorcism was arranged. Two local priests, Father Raymond Bishop and Father William Bowdern, performed the rite. The exorcism began on March 16, 1949. According to a diary Father Bishop kept, Robbie "was seized violently so that he began to struggle with his pillow and the bed clothing. . . . The contortions revealed physical strength beyond the natural power. . . . He fought and screamed in a diabolical, high-pitched voice."[31] The priests continued to pray and placed blessed objects on Robbie's body, but the boy's suffering continued.

On April 18—the day after Easter—the exorcists finally broke through. At 10:45 P.M., a booming voice emanated from Robbie: "I command you Satan, and the other evil spirits to leave the body in the name of **Dominus**. Immediately!"[32] After several minutes of what the diary calls "the most violent contortions of the entire period of exorcism," Robbie calmed down and said simply, "He's gone."[33] Later, Robbie described a vision of the archangel Michael driving the devil out of him.

Robbie went on to live a normal life, never speaking of the ritual that freed him from possession. If any official records of the exorcism exist, they are hidden away under lock and key. The diary kept during the ritual is the only record of this extraordinary event—that, plus a film that scared countless moviegoers and brought the ancient rite of exorcism into popular culture.

Notes

Chapter 1: Possessed by Spirits

1. Carl Sagan, *The Demon-Haunted World: Science as a Candle in the Dark.* New York: Ballantine, 1996, p. 115.
2. Quoted in Edith Fiore, *The Unquiet Dead: A Psychologist Treats Spirit Possession.* Garden City, NY: Doubleday, 1987, p. 16.
3. Matthew 15:22, *The Holy Bible, New International Version.* Grand Rapids, MI: Zondervan, 1978, p. 1053.
4. Quoted in AllExperts Encyclopedia, "Salem Witch Trials." http://en.allexperts.com/e/s/sa/salem_witch_trials.htm.
5. Quoted in Kenneth P. Minkema, "'The Devil Will Roar in Me Anon': The Possession of Martha Roberson, Boston, 1741," in *Spellbound: Women and Witchcraft in America*, ed. Elizabeth Reis. Wilmington, DE: Scholarly Resources, 1998, p. 100.
6. Quoted in Minkema, "'The Devil Will Roar in Me Anon,'" p. 101.
7. Robert Todd Carroll, "Exorcism," *The Skeptic's Dictionary.* http://skepdic.com/exorcism.html.

Chapter 2: Contacting the Spirit World

8. Quoted in DC Pages.com, "Abraham Lincoln's Ghost." www.dcpages.com/Events/Holidays/Halloween/Abraham _Lincoln.shtml.
9. Quoted in Carl Sandburg, *Abraham Lincoln: The Prairie Years and the War Years.* New York: Harcourt, Brace, 1954, p. 394.
10. Quoted in Casper S. Yost, *Patience Worth: A Psychic Mystery.* New York: Henry Holt, 1916, p. 2.
11. Quoted in Ramtha's School of Enlightenment, "JZ Knight, the Channel." www.ramtha.com/html/aboutus/about-jz.stm#who.
12. Quoted in Editors of Time-Life Books, *Spirit Summonings.* Alexandria, VA: Time-Life Books, 1989, p. 141.
13. Ramtha, "The Gift of Love." http://ramtha.com/html/ community/teachings/giftoflove.pdf.

Chapter 3: Cases of Possession

14. "The Possession of Elizabeth Knapp." http://homepages. rootsweb.com/~sam/knapp/elizabeth.html.
15. Quoted in David D. Hall, "Witch Hunting in Salem," *Christian History* 13, no. 1 (2001). www.christianitytoday.com/ holidays/halloween/features/salem.html.
16. Quoted in Hall, "Witch Hunting in Salem."
17. Quoted in Hall, "Witch Hunting in Salem."
18. Quoted in Monstrous.com, "The Watseka Wonder." http://ghosts.monstrous.com/the_watseka_wonder.htm.
19. Quoted in Troy Taylor, *Haunted Illinois*. Alton, IL: Whitechapel Productions, 1999, p. 216.
20. Quoted in Monstrous.com, "The Watseka Wonder."
21. Quoted in Malachi Martin, *Hostage to the Devil: The Possession and Exorcism of Five Living Americans*. New York: Reader's Digest, 1976, p. 263.
22. Quoted in Martin, *Hostage to the Devil*, p. 273.
23. Quoted in Martin, *Hostage to the Devil*, p. 274.
24. Quoted in Martin, *Hostage to the Devil*, p. 282.
25. Quoted in Martin, *Hostage to the Devil*, p. 256.

Chapter 4: Freeing the Possessed

26. Quoted in Erin Randolph, "Begone Satan," *City View*, October 13, 2005. www.dmcityview.com/archives/ oct/10-13-05/cover.shtml.
27. Quoted in Celestine Kaspner, "Begone Satan!" ETWN Library: New Age and Cults. www.ewtn.com/library/NEW AGE /BEGONESA.htm.
28. Quoted in Kaspner, "Begone Satan!"
29. Quoted in MoviesOnline, "Emily Rose: The Real Story of Anneliese Michel's Exorcism." www.moviesonline.ca/movie news_1253.html.
30. Quoted in Thomas B. Allen, *Possessed: The True Story of an Exorcism*. New York: Doubleday, 1993, p. 33.
31. Quoted in Chad Garrison, "Hell of a House," *St. Louis Riverfront Times*, October 26, 2005. www.rftstl.com/ 2005-10-26/news/hell-of-a-house/3.
32. Quoted in Allen, *Possessed*, p. 192.
33. Quoted in Allen, *Possessed*, p. 192.

Glossary

archaic: Old-fashioned.

benign: Not harmful.

Dominus: Latin for "Lord."

epilepsy: A disease of the brain that causes involuntary muscle contractions (seizures).

exorcism: A religious ritual used to remove a demon from a possessed person.

gullible: Easily deceived.

parapsychology: The study of events that cannot be explained by science or physical laws.

psychic: Outside of natural or known physical processes.

skeptics: People who doubt or question what others accept as fact.

superstitious: Believing in spells, omens, or magic rather than in science or the laws of nature.

trance: A sleeplike state during which a person's body may be used by spirits.

For Further Exploration

Books

Robert Gardner, *What's So Super About the Supernatural?* Brookfield, CT: Twenty-first Century, 1998. Includes information and activities related to various paranormal phenomena.

Stuart A. Kallen, *Possessions and Exorcisms.* Detroit: Lucent, 2005. An in-depth look at the phenomenon of possession and its various forms.

Patricia D. Netzley, *Paranormal Phenomena.* San Diego: Lucent, 2000. An overview of mysterious and unexplained occurrences.

Web Sites

"Demon," Encyclopedia at Kids.Net.Au (http://encyclo pedia.kids.net.au/page/de/Demon). This article gives basic information about demons and includes several links to other demon-related pages.

Exorcism: Driving Out the Nonsense, *Skeptical Inquirer* (http://www.csicop.org/si/2001–01/i-files.html). Presents a skeptical examination of the story behind *The Exorcist* movie.

Psychic Phenomena, About.com (http://paranormal. about.com/od/psychicphenomena/Psychic_Phenom ena.htm). This site contains links to information about channeling, Ouija boards, and other unexplained phenomena.

Index

Picture Credits

About the Author

Craig E. Blohm has written numerous magazine articles and books for young readers. This is his first book for KidHaven Press. A Chicago native, Blohm lives with his wife, Desiree, in Tinley Park, Illinois.